CW01308527

Elaina Moon

Copyright © Elaina Moon 2025

ISBN 978-1-0683515-1-8

www.elainamoon.com

Kalyke Books

THIS BOOK BELONGS TO:

Inspired by the 200th anniversary of the modern railway and a family trip to Hopetown Darlington.

Amelia is an inventor!

At five years old, Amelia built houses, stables, cars, trains, ships, planes and rockets using plastic bottles, pieces of cardboard, and anything else she could find in the recycling box.

At nine years old, Amelia designed and built her first robot and she called him Stanley.

Amelia (Age 5)

Amelia (Age 9)

Amelia designed and built many things with Stanley. But the best invention was a pair of Time Travelling Trainers!

They used the trainers to travel back in time to meet famous inventors.

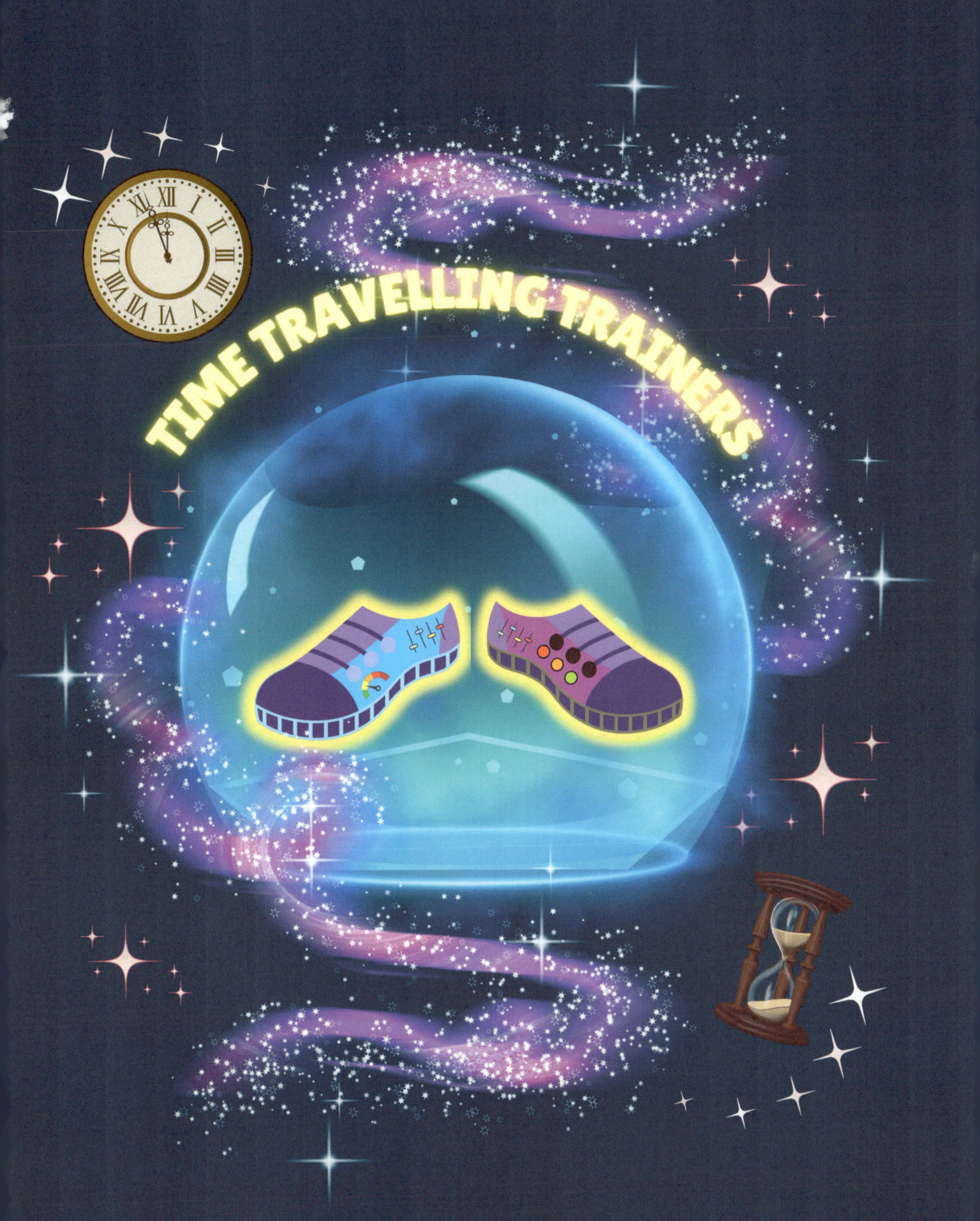

TIME TRAVELLING TRAINERS

After visiting Hopetown with her family, and seeing the magnificent replica of 'Locomotion', Amelia wanted to know everything about it. She wanted to know who built it, where they built it, how they built it and why it was such an important invention.

'Locomotion'

Wagon

Coach

But where to start?

From her visit to Hopetown, Amelia had learned that 'Locomotion' was built in Newcastle upon Tyne at the Robert Stephenson and Company workshop. The company was the World's first factory especially designed to build locomotives.

ROBERT STEPHENSON & Co.

JUNE 1823

NEWCASTLE ON TYNE

LOCOMOTION

So who better to speak to than Robert Stephenson himself?

Excited, Amelia set her Time Travelling Trainers to transport her and Stanley back to 1825 and the grand opening of the Stockton and Darlington Railway.

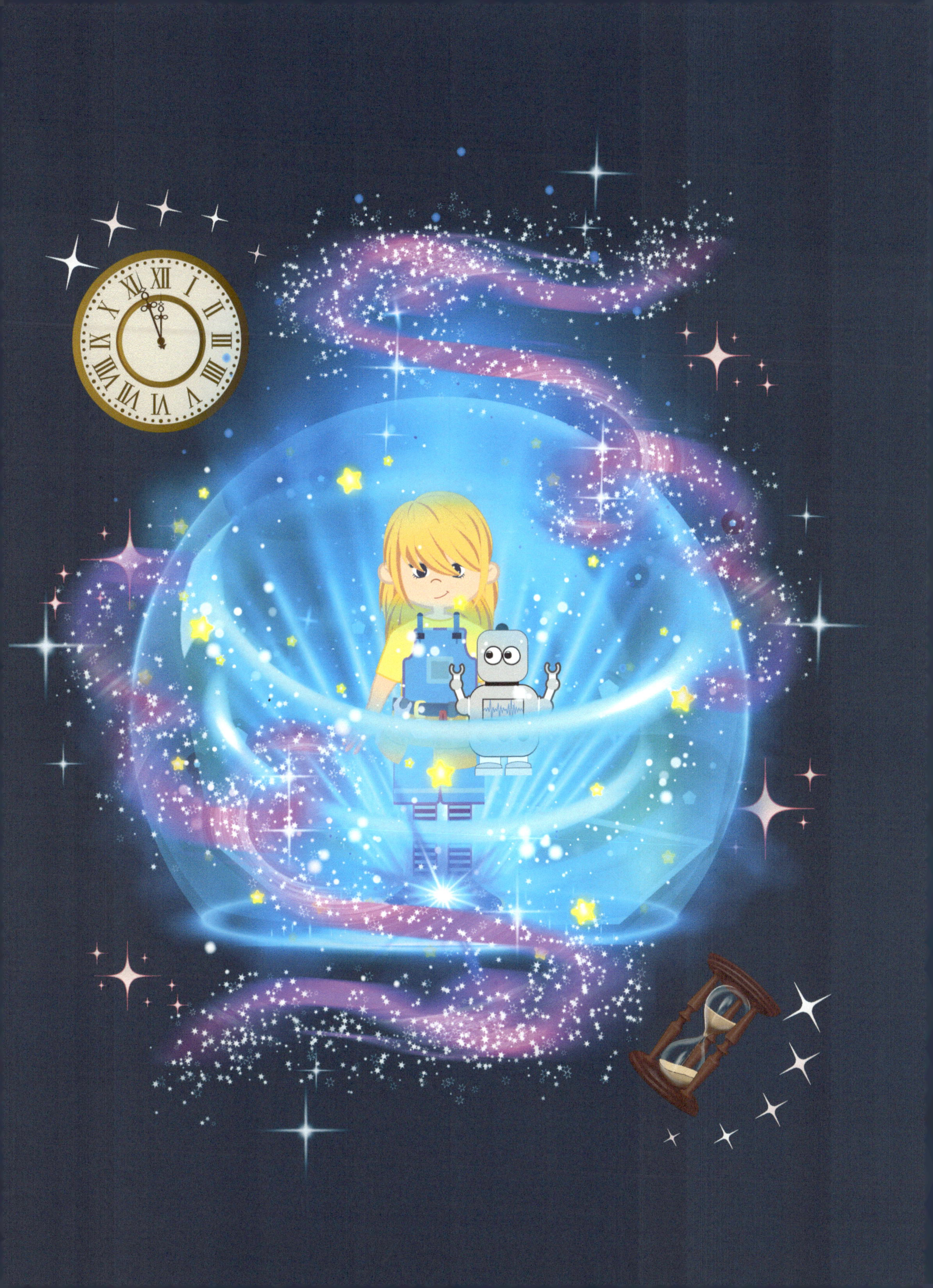

Amelia and Stanley arrived in Shildon and headed straight over to see Robert Stephenson.

Robert was pleased to see the young engineer and her little robot. He realised quite quickly that Amelia had many questions and he was happy to answer them all. Robert began by giving a tour of 'Locomotion', the wagons, and the luxury coach called 'Experiment'.

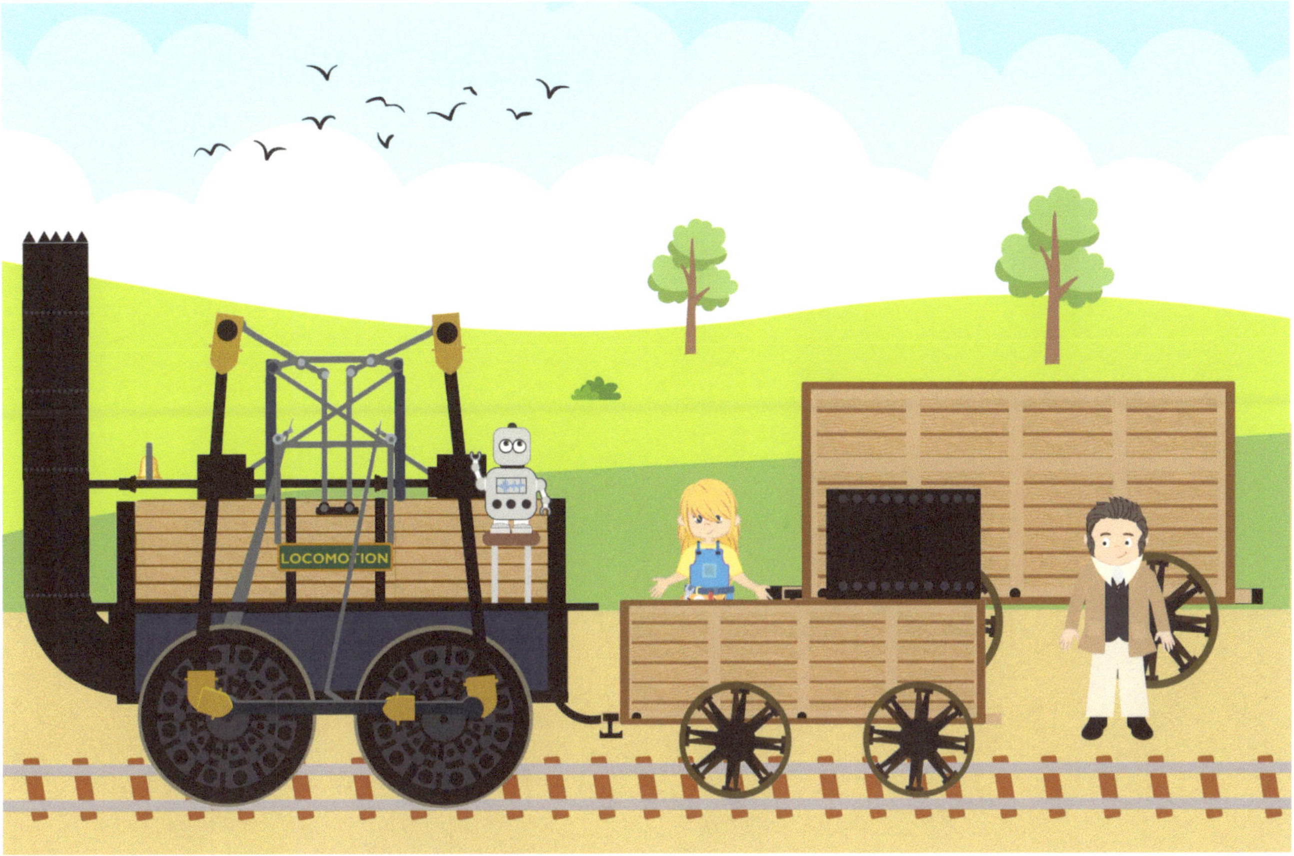
LOCOMOTION

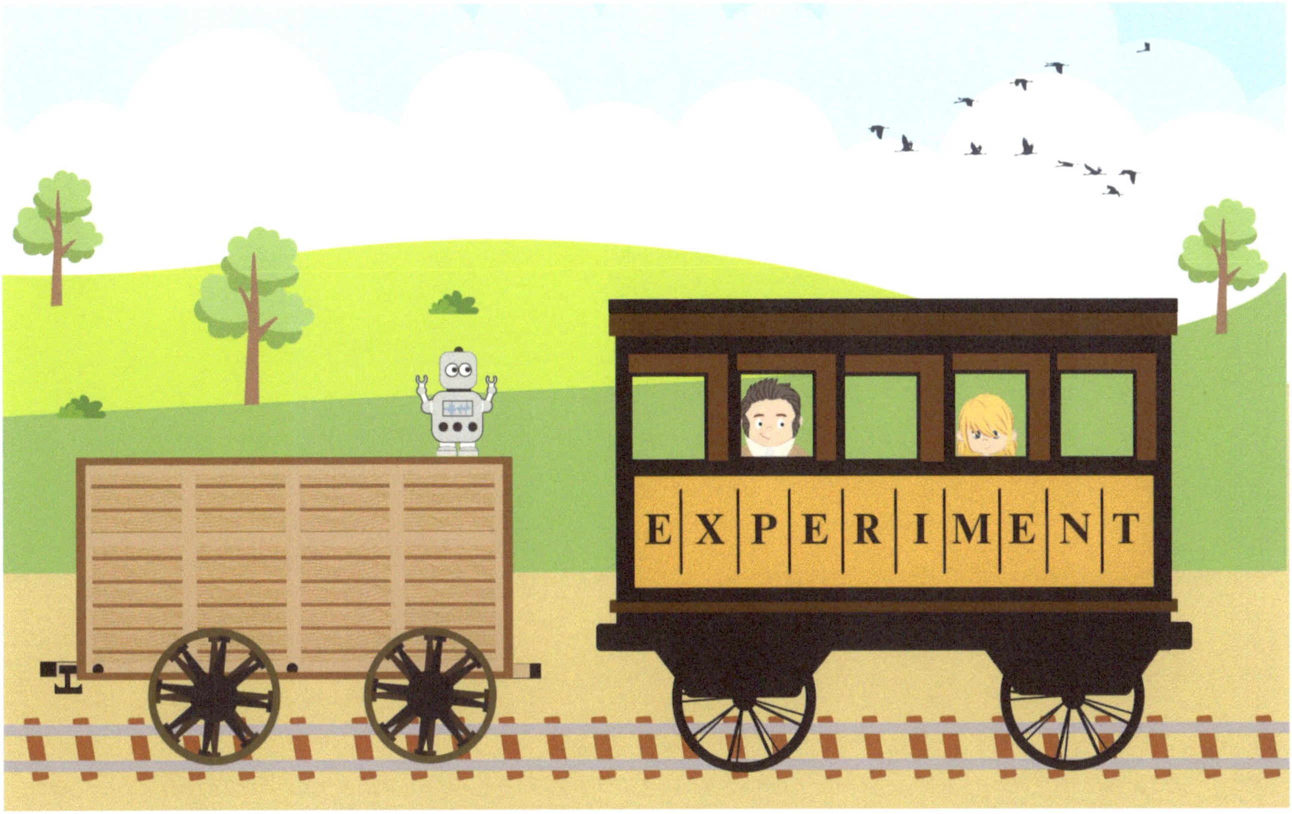
EXPERIMENT

He explained that to get 'Locomotion' all the way from Newcastle to Shildon before the big opening day, it had to be taken apart in the workshop and carried on three horse-drawn wagons to Aycliffe Lane Railway Station. It was then carefully put back together and placed on the railway tracks.

ROBERT STEPHENSON & Co.
JUNE 1823
NEWCASTLE ON TYNE

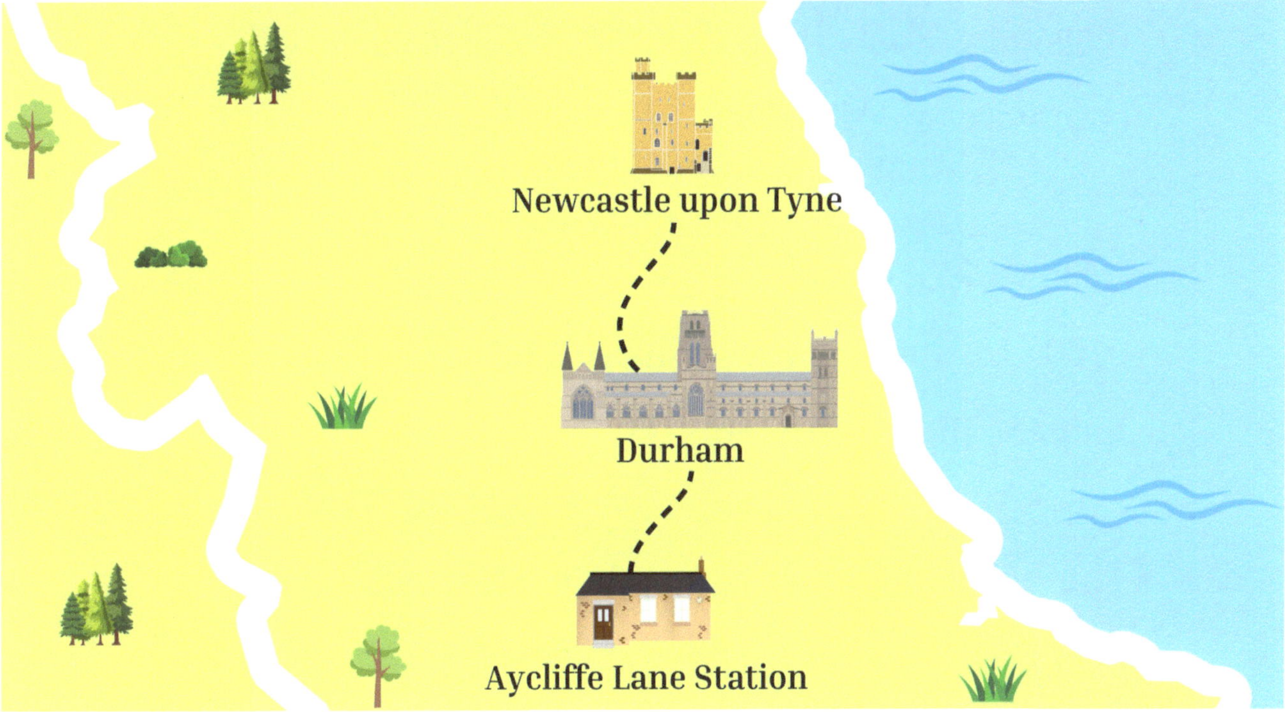
Newcastle upon Tyne
Durham
Aycliffe Lane Station

LOCOMOTION

Robert told Amelia and Stanley that the Stockton and Darlington Railway was built to transport coal from the Durham coal mines to the Port of Stockton.

Coal was in great demand because it was used to fuel trains, ships and factories, heat homes and power lights.

The coal would be taken by rail to the docks on the quayside of the River Tees and then loaded onto ships and delivered to other parts of the country.

Witton Park Coal Mine

Stockton and Darlington Railway

Shildon

Darlington

Stockton

Stockton Quayside

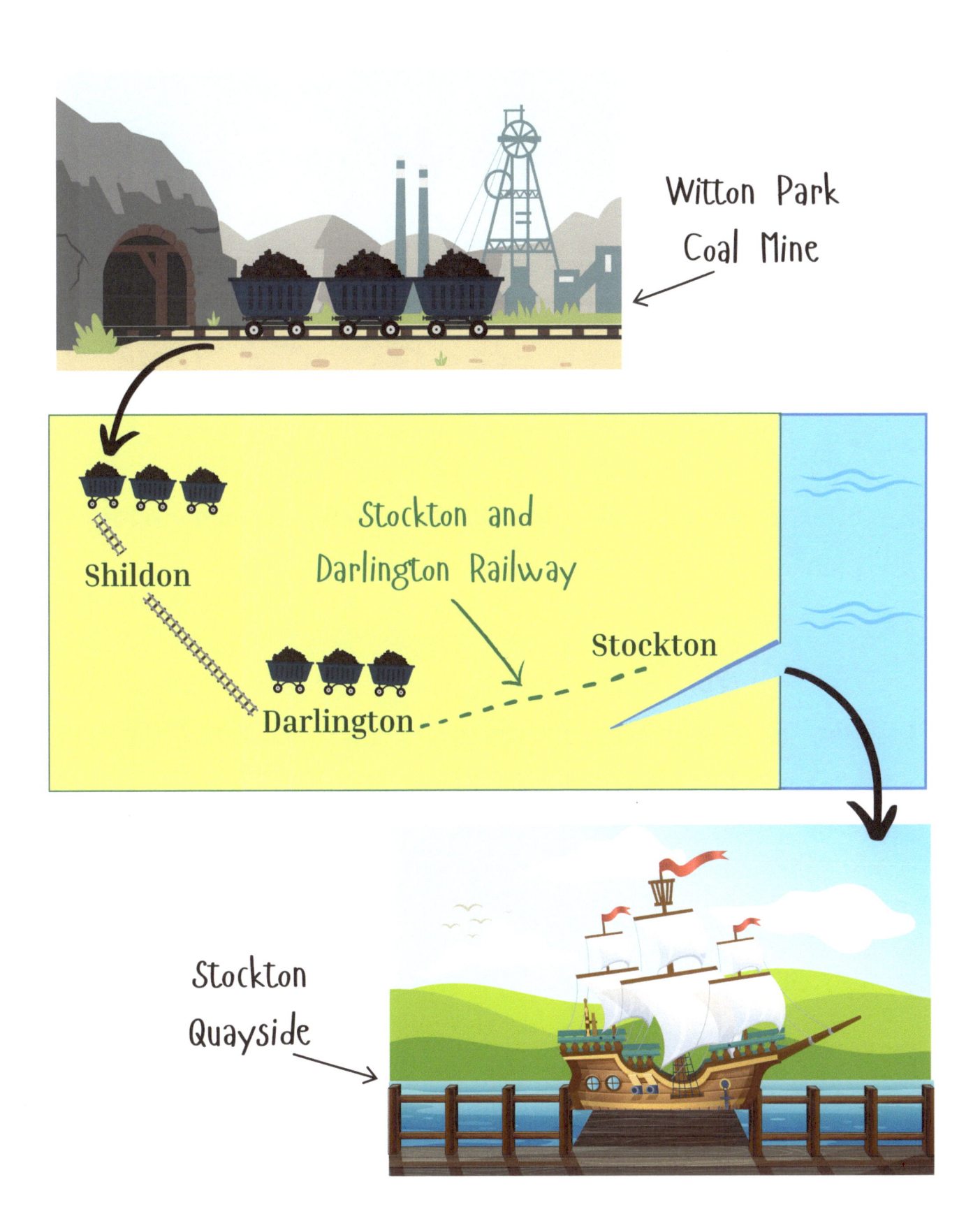

Edward Pease was the main supporter of the new Stockton and Darlington Railway and had planned to use horses to pull the wagons.

But Robert's father, George Stephenson, convinced him that a steam engine could pull 50 times the weight horses could and travel more quickly.

So, Edward chose George to be his Chief Engineer, and along with Robert, was put in charge of designing and building the steam locomotive for the new railway line.

George, a pioneering railway engineer, used his experience of building steam locomotives at Killingworth Colliery to design 'Locomotion'.

Coal was burned in the firebox and the hot gas in the flue tube heated the water in the boiler until it turned into steam.

Steam from the boiler was squeezed into the cylinders, making the pistons move.

The movement of the pistons pushed the connecting rods attached to the wheels, making the train move along.

The hot gas passed through the flue tube and out of the chimney as smoke.

Improvements were made to the design of this new locomotive, making it the first to have coupling rods, linking the driving wheels to stop them from slipping on the iron rails.

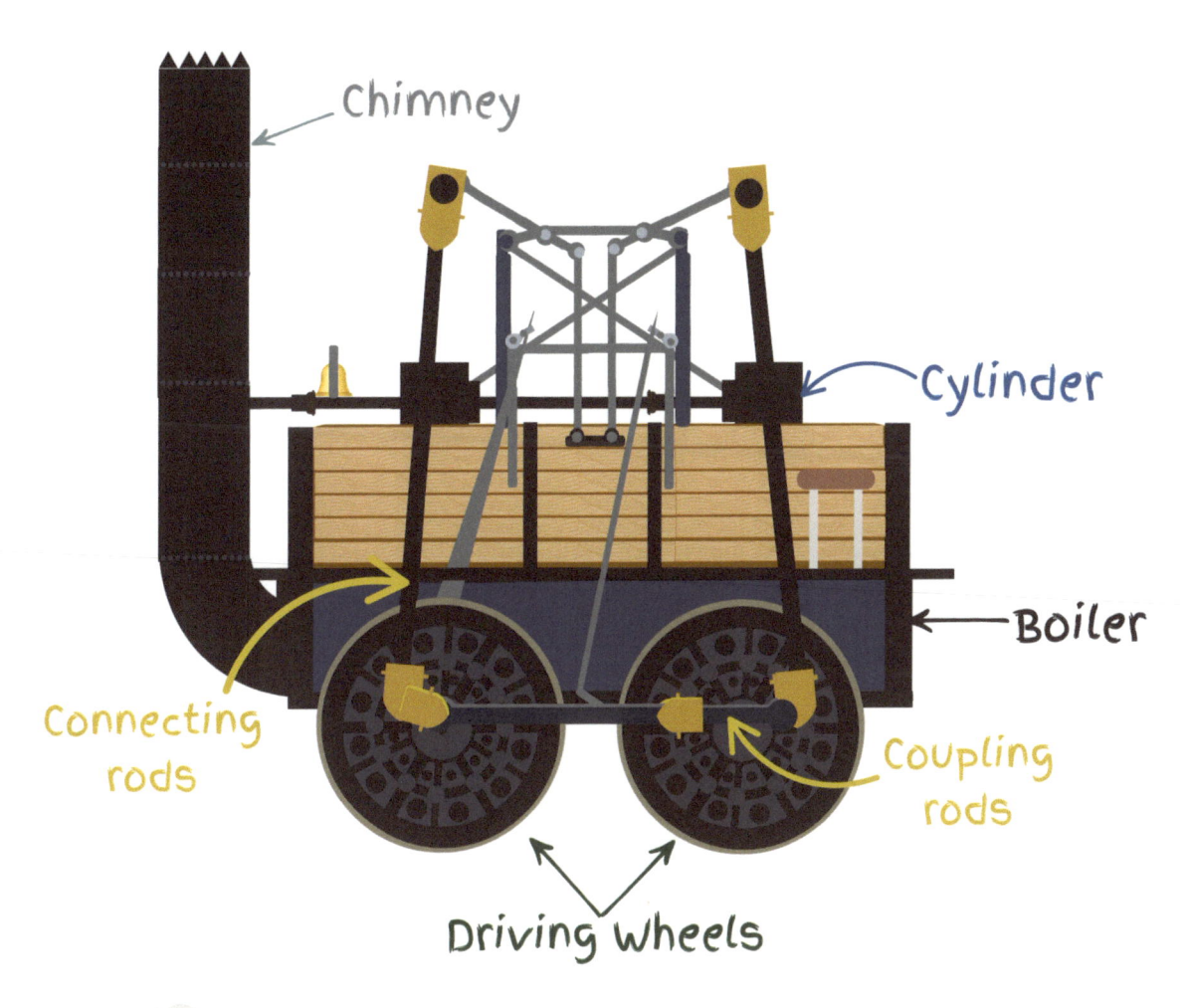

Chimney

Cylinder

Boiler

Connecting rods

Coupling rods

Driving Wheels

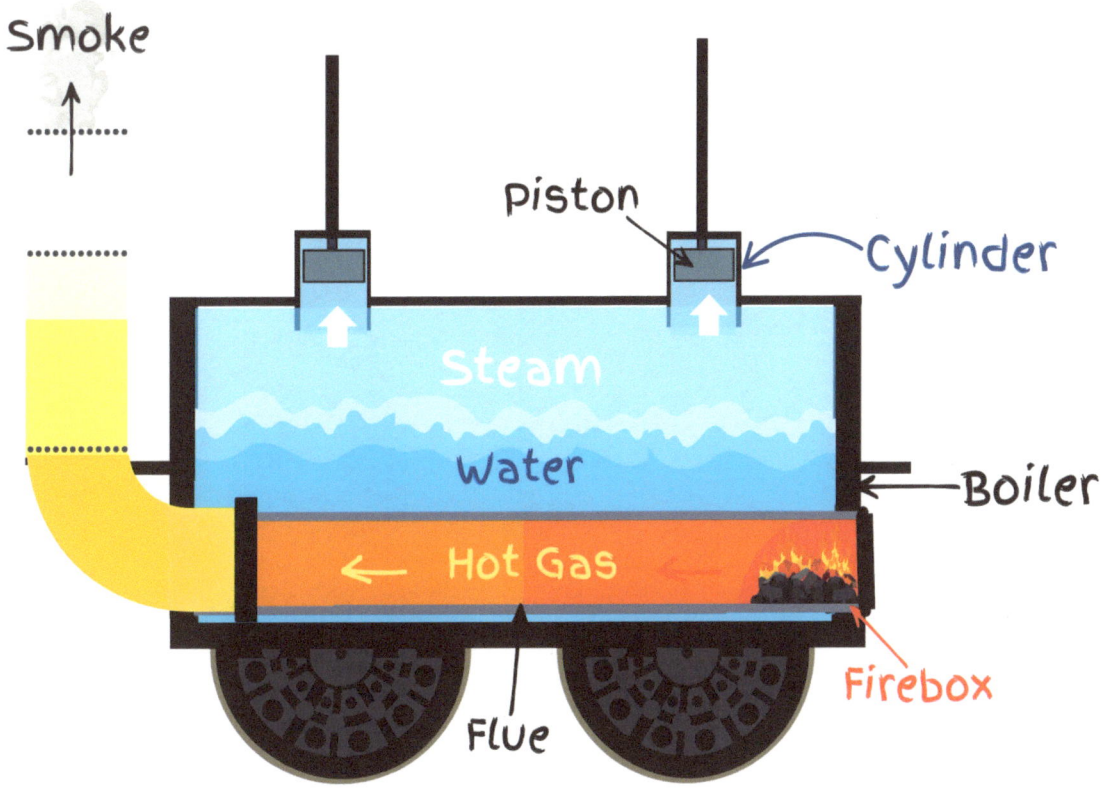

Smoke

Piston

Cylinder

Steam

Water

Boiler

Hot Gas

Firebox

Flue

By the time of the grand opening of the railway, 'Locomotion' was designed to pull wagons and coaches to transport coal, flour, and passengers between Darlington and Stockton.

George was to be the driver of the train, the fireman would feed the firebox with coal and the railway workers were to be positioned between each wagon ready to pull the brakes if needed.

Coal

flour

Passengers

Businessmen

EXPERIMENT

George Stephenson

Fireman

Railway worker

27th September 1825

On the morning of the big day, the fireman lit the firebox using a magnifying glass to create sparks (because matches had not been invented yet!).

Amelia and Robert boarded the special luxury coach, while George drove the train to Stockton, passing over Skerne Bridge along the way.

300 tickets were sold for the first historical ride on the steam train, but 600 people squeezed into the wagons and even sat on the wagons already carrying coal.

When the train arrived in Stockton, there were lots of celebrations, with a 21-gun salute and a brass band-led procession to the Town Hall for a grand banquet.

'Locomotion' became the very first steam locomotive to carry passengers on a public railway.

Amelia and Stanley had a wonderful time. But all too soon, it was time for them to say goodbye to Robert Stephenson and head home.

Although they were sad to leave 1825 and the opening of the Stockton and Darlington Railway, they were excited to return to the inventing room to write about their adventure.

Amelia and Stanley drew pictures of 'Locomotion', the wagons and the luxury coach.

They built a model of Skerne Bridge and recreated the journey they made riding on the first steam train to take passengers on the Stockton and Darlington Railway.

Amelia and Stanley took a trip to see Robert Stephenson.

1825

As for Robert, he went on to improve the steam locomotive, designing the famous 'Rocket' in 1829.

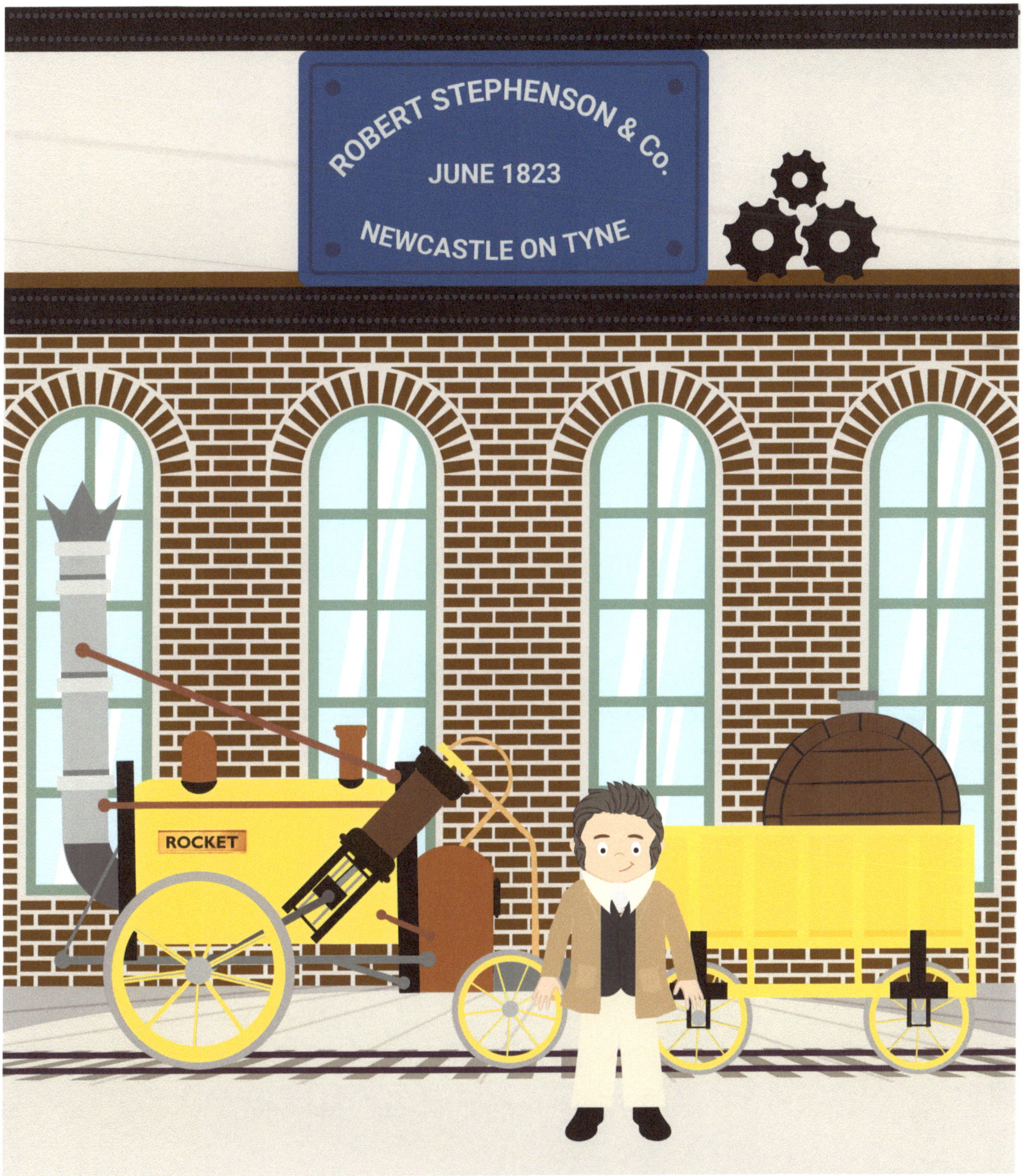
ROBERT STEPHENSON & Co.
JUNE 1823
NEWCASTLE ON TYNE
ROCKET

FUN FACTS

'Locomotion' was called 'Active' when it was first built, but it was later changed to 'Locomotion Number One'.

Aycliffe Lane Station is now called Heighington Station.

Not everyone was happy about the new railway, especially the Earl of Darlington who didn't want it to go through his land. He even attempted to bankrupt the Stockton and Darlington Railway Company!

Skerne Bridge was built in 1825 for the Stockton and Darlington Railway. It is now the oldest railway bridge in continuous use in the World.

On the 27th of September 1825, 'Locomotion' pulled 35 wagons and 1 luxury coach at a speed of up to 12 miles per hour.

Crowds of 40,000 people arrived from all over the country to watch the opening of the railway.

If you would like to learn more about 'Locomotion' and George and Robert Stephenson, there are many places you can visit.

Hopetown Darlington
www.hopetowndarlington.co.uk

Locomotion
www.locomotion.org.uk

National Railway Museum
www.railwaymuseum.org.uk

Beamish
www.beamish.org.uk

Robert Stephenson Trust
www.robertstephensontrust.com

Stephenson Steam Railway Museum
www.stephensonsteamrailway.org.uk

AVAILABLE NOW

To find out more about Stephenson's Rocket, take another trip with Amelia and Stanley, this time back to 1829, the year of the Rainhill Trials.

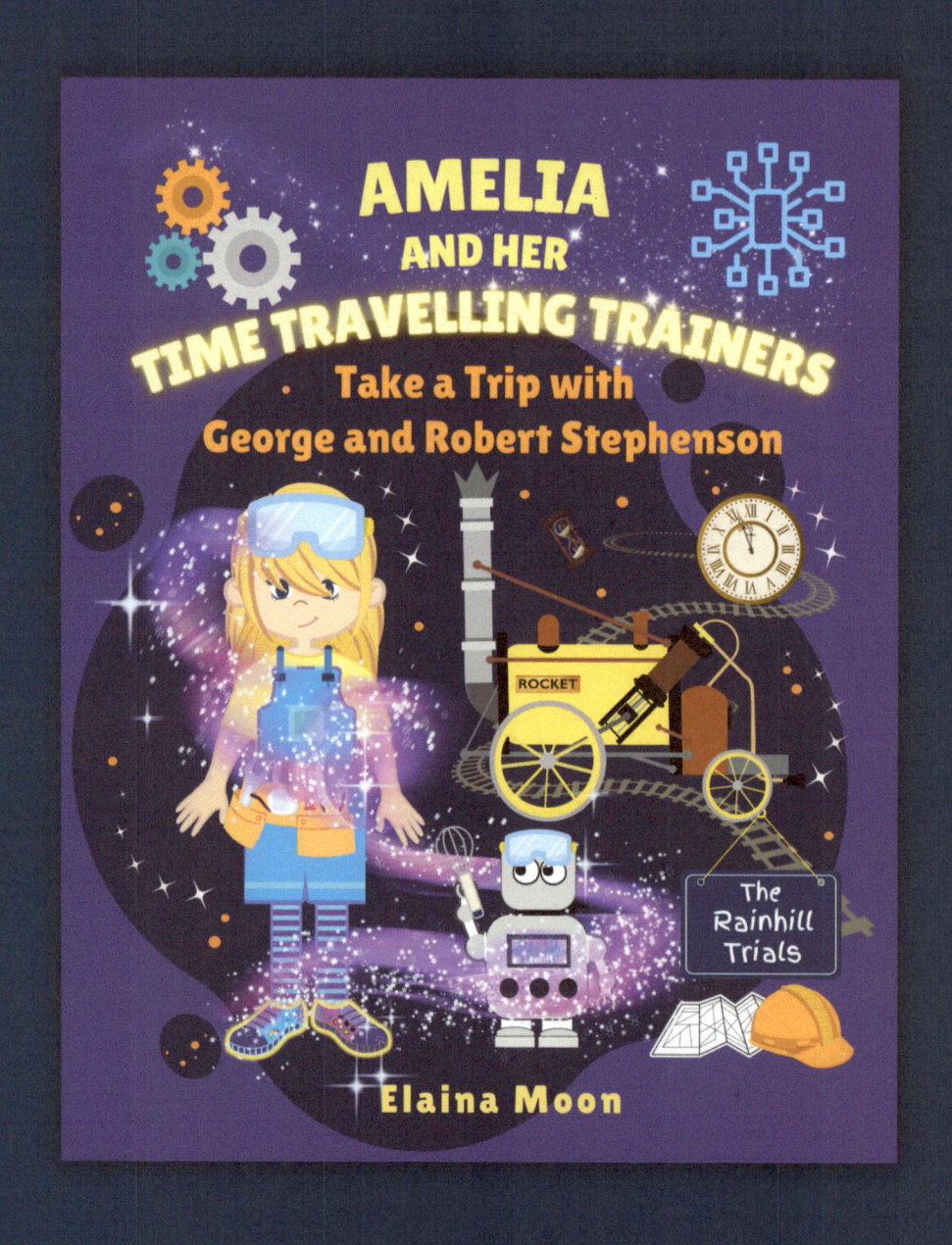

www.elainamoon.com